I CAN, TOO

Senior Authors
Carl B. Smith
Virginia A. Arnold

Linguistics Consultant
Ronald Wardhaugh

Macmillan Publishing Co., Inc.
New York

Collier Macmillan Publishers
London

ACKNOWLEDGMENTS

The publisher gratefully acknowledges permission to reprint the following copyrighted material:

"At the Zoo" from *Whispers and Other Poems* by Myra Cohn Livingston. Copyright © 1958 by Myra Cohn Livingston. Reprinted by permission of Marian Reiner for the author.

"Catch a Little Rhyme" from *Catch a Little Rhyme* by Eve Merriam. Copyright © 1966 by Eve Merriam. Reprinted by permission of the author.

"The Park" from *Crickety Cricket! The Best-Loved Poems of James S. Tippett.* Copyright © 1973 by Martha K. Tippett. Reprinted by permission of Harper & Row, Publishers, Inc. Published in the UK and British Commonwealth by World's Word Ltd. and reprinted also with their permission.

Illustrations: Ray Cruz, pp. 2-3; Susan Lexa, pp. 4-11; Bill Davis, pp. 26-35; Olivia Cole, pp. 36-37; Sal Murdoca, pp. 38-47; Jan Pyk, pp. 48-57; Lionel Kalish, pp. 58-61; Olivia Cole, pp. 62-63. **Photographs:** Sonja Bullaty, pp. 12-13; Charles Palek and Kojo Tanaka/Animals, Animals, p. 14; George Ancona, pp. 15-23 (Special thanks to the Metro Zoo, Zoological Society of Florida, Miami Seaquarium, and Parrot Jungle of Miami, Florida, for their cooperation.); Miriam Austermall/Animals, Animals, pp. 24-25. **Cover Design:** Jan Pyk.

Macmillan Publishing Co., Inc.
866 Third Avenue, New York, New York 10022
Collier Macmillan Canada, Inc.

Printed in the United States of America
ISBN 0-02-131670-8
98

Contents

HATS

Harriet Ziefert

The boys and girls are at the park.
The little boy calls to the little girl.
He likes that hat.

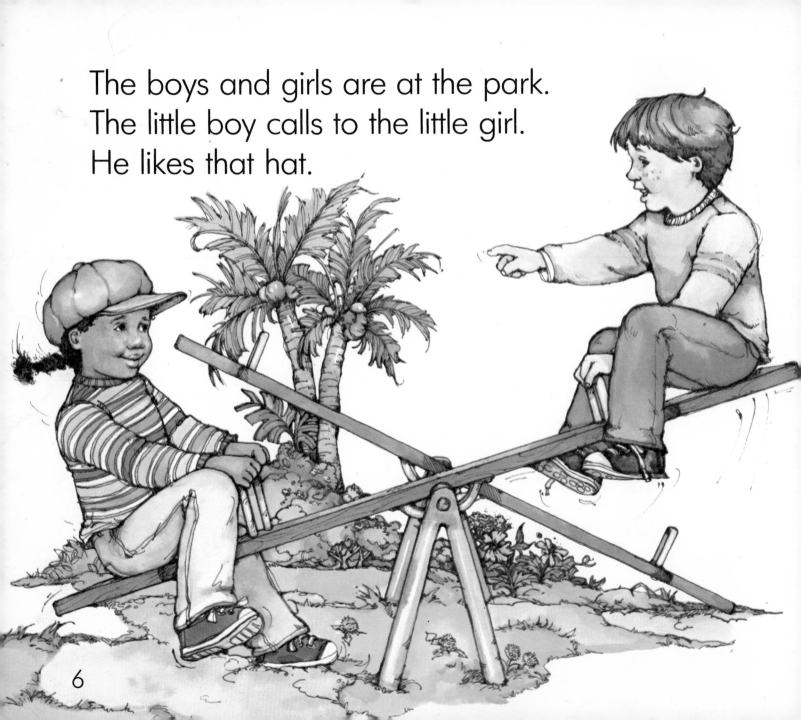

The big girl calls to the big boy.
The girl likes that hat.

The little boy and the big girl are sad.
Why are the boy and the girl sad?

A man is at the park.
The man rides down the hill.
A dog is at the park, too.
The dog jumps down the hill.
Now the hats go down the hill.

The hats go down the hill.
Little hats and big hats go down.
The boy and the girl see the hats.

The boy likes the hat.
The girl likes the hat.
The dog likes the hat, too.
Are the boy and the girl sad now?

The Park

I'm glad that I
   Live near a park

For in the winter
   After dark

The park lights shine
   As bright and still

As dandelions
   On a hill.

—James S. Tippett

THE ZOO

Bette Davidson Kalash

Kate likes to go to the zoo.
Kate likes to walk and look.

Who is that man?
Why does he walk in?
Why can't Kate walk in, too?

Kate likes birds.
Kate can read the word <u>birds</u>.
Kate can walk in to see the birds.

Filmed at the Parrot Jungle, Miami, Florida.

Kate can see a little bird.
Can you see the little bird?
Kate can see a big bird, too.

Boys and girls can ride at the zoo.
Kate likes to ride, too.

Kate likes to go up and ride.
Now Kate can look down.
Girls and boys look little now.

In the zoo is a little zoo.
Boys and girls like the little zoo.
Kate likes the little zoo, too.

Who likes the zoo?
Kate does!

AT THE ZOO

I've been to the zoo
   where the thing that you do
is watching the things
that the animals do—

and watching
   the animals
   all watching
         you!

—Myra Cohn Livingston

Ben and the Fish

Ben walks and walks.
He walks down to the lake.

28

Ben likes to sit and fish.
Ben likes words, too.
He likes to read.

Now it rains at the lake.
Where do the words go?
Ben can't see the words.

Where can Ben go now?
It rains and rains at the lake.
Ben can't fish and read.

Ben walks to the house.
He calls Nan.
Nan likes to look at fish.

It rains and rains.
Nan walks to the house.
Where can Ben and Nan see fish?

Fish are in the house!
Where do Ben and Nan see fish
in the house?

Look at the fish!
Ben and Nan **do** like fish!

35

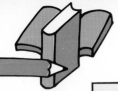

Ending Sounds

Hear	Read	Write
	man bird	__man__

   Ben   big   1. _____

   hat   sad   2. _____

   dog   read   3. _____

   word   down   4. _____

36

Read	 Write
[t | **g**] The do__ can jump.	*The dog can jump.*

[n \| d]   1. Be__ likes to fish.

[d \| t]   2. He can fish a__ the lake.

[g \| t]   3. Tha__ is a little bird.

[d \| g]   4. The dog can see the bir__.

[g \| d]   5. The bi__ dog jumps.

THE CAR

Sally Bell

The man sees the city.
He walks and walks.

The man sees a big car.
He sees a little car.

Now I have the hat and the car.

The man rides out of the city.
He rides in the little car
to the house.

47

THE
AND
FUNNY

BUS
THE
THINGS

The bus says, "I go up the hill.
I go down the hill.
Ride now!"

A man runs.
He runs up the hill.
He runs up to the bus.

The man calls,
"Do you go down the hill?
Can I ride down the hill?
Can the funny things ride
down the hill, too?"

The bus says, "I go down the hill.
I can see you, but where are
the funny things?
What are the funny things?"

A big dog and a little dog run to the bus.
The bus says, "I see the dogs.
I can't see the funny things.
Are the funny things like dogs?"

The man says, "Dogs can run,
but the funny things can't run.
The funny things can jump."

Now the bus sees the funny things.

"The funny things **can** jump!"
says the bus.

The bus says, "I like the funny things.
Can the funny things ride?"

The funny things call,
"We can ride!
We can ride!"

"Jump in," calls the bus.
The funny things jump in.
The man jumps in, too.

The bus says, "We can go
down the hill now."

The funny things ride
in the bus.
The funny things call out,
"We can ride in the bus!
We like the bus!"

Catch a Little Rhyme

Once upon a time
I caught a little rhyme

I set it on the floor
but it ran right out the door

I chased it on my bicycle
but it melted to an icicle

I scooped it up in my hat
but it turned into a cat

I caught it by the tail
but it stretched into a whale

I followed it in a boat
but it changed into a goat

When I fed it tin and paper
it became a tall skyscraper

Then it grew into a kite
and flew far out of sight . . .

—Eve Merriam

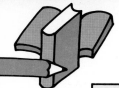

Vowel Sounds

 Hear	Read	Write
(cup)	dog r<u>u</u>n	__run__

 bus   hill   1. _____

 that   little   2. _____

 runs   down   3. _____

 sad   jump   4. _____

62

 Read	 Write
u / a You are in a b__s.	You are in a bus.

u / a	1. What c__n you see?
u / a	2. You can see th__t park.
u / a	3. See a girl j__mp.
u / a	4. A m__n jumps, too.
u / a	5. A boy r__ns.

WORD LIST

6. are	look	do	48. funny
hat	19. bird	38. car	49. bus
8. sad	27. Ben	39. city	things
9. hill	28. lake	40. what	50. says
16. zoo	30. it	42. have	53. run
Kate	rains	or	55. we
walk	where	45. lost	

To the Teacher: The words listed beside the page numbers above are instructional-vocabulary words introduced in *I Can, Too*.

4. hats	18. birds	29. words	50. runs
6. at	28. walks	39. sees	

To the Teacher: The children should be able to independently identify the applied-skills words listed beside the page numbers above by using previously taught phonics skills or by recognizing derived forms of words previously introduced.